Chinese Pioneering Inventions Series

Canals

Edited by Li Chaodong

Translated by Xuemeng Angela Li

Books Beyond Boundaries

ROYAL COLLINS

Where did ancient humans live? What do their habitats have in common?

If you look closely at the geographical location of the four oldest civilizations, you will find that ancient humans inhabited nearby rivers.

Since China is one of the four oldest civilizations, it also originated from rivers.

Human beings cannot survive without water. Therefore, ancient humans gradually settled near rivers, gathered into different tribes, and developed civilization. It can be concluded that the river is the source of human civilization.

The topography of China is high in the west and low in the east. As a result, most of the rivers in China flow from west to east as water flows downwards.

Rivers are all located in different areas where climate varies. But climate remains consistent within one river basin, which leads to similar products across the basin. In contrast, there is a huge difference between the produce of north and south China. The main crop of regions around the middle and lower reaches of the Yangtze River is rice, while wheat and millet are the main crops grown in the Yellow River basin.

There are many rivers in Jiangnan (the south region of the lower reaches of the Yangtze River), resulting in a moist climate and high crop yield across the region. However, the political centers of ancient China were mainly located in its northern regions, where the amount of food was relatively limited for the size of the population. Hence, it was necessary to transport food from the south to the north.

But it was very inconvenient to transport food to the north. In ancient China, there were few roads with difficult walking conditions. Food was normally transported on land by walking, wagons, or oxcarts. It would then be unloaded by a riverbank to be reloaded on board for transportation via water. Once the river ended, people had to unload the food again and then continued transporting it by walking, wagons, or oxcarts.

Such a process must be repeated many times for food and other goods to reach the north. It not only consumes tremendous labor but is also inefficient.

The grain hasn't arrived yet?
The journey is far, the amount of grain is large, and transportation is troublesome. If transported by boat, although the speed is not as fast as horses, the capacity is large, the transportation cost is low, but not all the way has a river.

In order to quickly and easily transport food from Jiangnan to the capital and strengthen his control over the region, Emperor Yang of the Sui Dynasty gave the order to open a canal.

If there is no river, then make a river!

Emperor Yang drafted millions of civilians to dig the **Tongji Canal**, which connects Luoyang and Huai'an City. More than 100,000 people dredged the **Hangou Canal** between Huai'an and Yangzhou. Three years later, millions of people were drafted again to dig the **Yongji Canal** that connects Luoyang to Beijing and the Jiangnan River between Zhenjiang and Hangzhou.

Finally, the **Grand Canal** was formed by connecting all four canals. It is more than 2,700 kilometers long and runs through China, connecting the north and south. Boats departing from Jiangnan can arrive directly at Luoyang by navigating the canal.

Upon the completion of the construction of the **Tongji Canal**, Emperor Yang immediately took a dragon boat to visit Jiangnan from Luoyang. At the time, at least 100,000 people accompanied him by boat. He also had cavalry escorting on both sides of the riverbanks, with 80,000 trackers pulling the boat forward. About 300,000 people participated in Emperor Yang's southern inspection tour.

Thousands of boats were mobilized for the tour. It had been more than 50 days after the departure of Emperor Yang's dragon boat when the last boat of the tour sailed out of Luoyang.

After the canal's opening, trade exchanges and cultural communications became more frequent, with cities springing up along the canal. Yangzhou was one of the most prosperous cities during the Tang Dynasty as the intersection of the Grand Canal and the Yangtze River.

Salt, iron, tea, silk, herbs, and porcelain were all shipped to Chang'an from Yangzhou, making Yangzhou a world-famous cosmopolitan city where goods from all over the world gathered. It was said that "Yangzhou is the top among all cities in the world" at the time.

Tongji Canal was called Bian River during the Northern Song Dynasty, of which the capital was Bianjing City (now Kaifeng). Grain and goods from different regions were all transported to Bianjing through the Bian River. Bianjing was the most prosperous and largest city in the world then. It had a vibrant commercial scene with more than 6,400 stores of relatively large scale and 8,000 to 9,000 peddlers.

After the opening of the Grand Canal, many granaries were set up along the canal and were mainly used for transiting grains. After grains were transported to Luoyang, it was stored in Huiluo Granary and Hanjia Granary, known as "The World's First Granary" at the time.

Zhenjiang, located at the confluence of the Yangtze River and the canal, also has many large granaries. Because the city has abundant grains, it makes vinegar using surplus grains. Zhenjiang vinegar has become one of the top four famous kinds of vinegar in China!

The Zhedong Canal was first built for irrigation purposes. As an extension of the Grand Canal, the Zhedong Canal connected the canal in the west and the Maritime Silk Road in the east. Many porcelains, teas, and silks products were shipped overseas through the Zhedong Canal.

Tanpeng Canal was a sea canal dug during the Tang Dynasty. After its opening, ships no longer had to take a detour at the Bailong Peninsula. They could reach Annam (now Vietnam) directly through the canal from the sea in Qinzhou, which created closer ties between China and Vietnam.

In fact, canals existed in China much earlier. But they were mostly used for military purposes in addition to food transportation.

The opening of the Hangou Canal was ordered by Fuchai, the King of Wu State. At that time, Fuchai wanted to go north to attack Qi, so he commanded people to open an artificial river channel from Yangzhou to divert the water of the Yangtze River into the Huai River, which connected both rivers and enabled the transportation of food and soldier through the waterway.

Similarly, Qin Shi Huang (the first emperor of the Qin Dynasty) ordered people to dig the Lingqu Canal to conquer the Nanyue Kingdom. The Lingqu Canal connected the Yangtze River water system to the Pearl River water system, allowing military reinforcements and food supplies to constantly reach the front line. It pushed forward the development of the war and played an important role in Qin Shi Huang's unification of Lingnan.

Upon the Yuan Dynasty, Kublai set Dadu (now Beijing) as its capital. Since the Sui-Tang Grand Canal was centered on Luoyang, transportation of grains always had to stop at Luoyang first before reaching Dadu. Thus, Kublai decided to open up a new channel.

Based on the original river channel, Jizhou Canal, Huitong Canal, and Tonghui Canal were opened during the Yuan Dynasty, transforming the canal course into a straight line running directly between north and south 900 kilometers shorter than before. The Beijing-Hangzhou Grand Canal that we know today was officially opened.

The opening of the Beijing-Hangzhou Grand Canal connected the Grand Canal with the Yangtze River, Gan River, Dayu Mountain, and Guangzhou City. This circulation route, known as the "Beijing-Guangzhou Grand Waterway," became an important transportation route for food and goods throughout the country, particularly during Ming and Qing dynasties.

After the Ming and Qing imposed a ban on maritime trade, Guangzhou was China's only foreign trade port for some time. The Thirteen Factories in Guangzhou, established during the Qing Dynasty, have grown into the logistics center for foreign trade, where Chinese and foreign goods are gathered. Guangzhou has thus become exceptionally prosperous.

During the Ming Dynasty, the government set up a governor in Huai'an that dedicates to managing national affairs on water transport of grains. The water transport of grains had a huge influence on fiscal revenue. During the Qing Dynasty, the tax revenue from the water transport of grains accounted for two-thirds of the government's fiscal revenue.

Qianlong Emperor also had as many as six southern inspection tours along the Beijing-Hangzhou Grand Canal. One of the purposes of the tour is to inspect the water conservancy projects along the canal. During the first southern inspection tour, more than 400 ships were mobilized, sometimes covering the entire surface of the river. Once they arrived in the Jiangnan area, bustling markets could be seen with countless stores which gathered diverse types of goods from all over the world.

Starting from the Jiaqing Emperor's era, grains' water transport began to decline as the canal riverbed became shallow. In conjunction with the corruption of officials and the failure of the canal system, the water transport of grains became increasingly outdated.

During the rule of the Daoguang Emperor, due to the blockage of the canal, the emperor ordered a trial of sea shipping that hired merchant ships to transfer the grains of Jiangnan to the capital via shipping lanes. The first sea shipping was a huge success.

In 1901 (the 27th Year of the Guangxu Emperor's rule), the Qing government ordered to stop the water transport of grains and converted all grains reserved for water transport into money, which finally put a closure to the water transport of grains in China. Later, due to the rise of railroads and the maturity of sea shipping, the Beijing-Hangzhou Grand Canal gradually declined.

Although the inland canals are no longer in use,
the sea canals play an important role.

The Panama Canal was opened for navigation in 1914. Previously, ships traveling between the east and west coasts of the United States had to take a detour through Cape Horn in South America. With the opening of the Panama Canal, the journey was shortened by about 15,000 kilometers.

Panama Canal
(It crosses the Isthmus of Panama and connects the Pacific and Atlantic Oceans.)

Suez Canal
(It runs through the Isthmus of Suez in Egypt and connects the Mediterranean Sea and the Red Sea.)

Opened in 1869, the Suez Canal is a major international shipping channel connecting Europe, Asia, and Africa. It shortened the voyage between the East and the West, one of the most frequently used routes in the world.

Both canals were not opened until the industrial civilization era. In contrast, China had canals more than 2,000 years ago. Opening a canal over 2,000 km long, more than 1,000 years ago. What a remarkable achievement that is!

Chinese Pioneering Inventions Series

Canals

Edited by Li Chaodong
Translated by Xuemeng Angela Li

First published in 2023 by Royal Collins Publishing Group Inc.
Groupe Publication Royal Collins Inc.
BKM Royalcollins Publishers Private Limited

Headquarters: 550-555 boul. René-Lévesque O Montréal (Québec) H2Z1B1 Canada
India office: 805 Hemkunt House, 8th Floor, Rajendra Place, New Delhi 110 008

Original Edition © Hohai University Press

ISBN: 978-1-4878-1101-3

To find out more about our publications, please visit www.royalcollins.com.

About the Editor

Li Chaodong, born in 1963, graduated from the Department of History of East China Normal University. He is a famous education publisher in China. He has edited and published more than 50 sets of books. He has won the title of "National Leading Talent in Press and Publication" and "China's Annual Publication Figure." He is the Founding Vice President of the All-China Federation of Industry and Commerce Book Industry Chamber of Commerce, Vice President of the Fifth Council of China Book Publishing Association, Vice Chairman of Anhui Publishing Association, and Vice Chairman of Jiangsu Publishing Association.